Agipt - Publishing

About Dr. Getan Eden:

Dr. Getan Eden is an African author who has dedicated his work to shedding light on the pressing issues of neo-colonialism and the exploitation of Africa's mineral wealth by global superpowers. With a deep passion for social justice and a keen understanding of the historical and contemporary challenges faced by the African continent, Dr. Eden has emerged as a prominent voice in advocating for the rights and liberation of African peoples.

With a strong academic background in political science and extensive research experience, Dr. Eden brings a nuanced and informed perspective to his writings. His works eloquently articulate the complex dynamics of neo-colonialism and highlight the multifaceted ways in which Africa's mineral wealth is exploited for the benefit of external powers, perpetuating cycles of inequality and hindering Africa's progress.

Dr. Eden's writings not only provide critical analysis but also offer solutions and avenues for change. Through his captivating prose, he navigates the intricate web of power relations, economic exploitation, and geopolitical interests that shape Africa's relationship with the world. By amplifying the voices of marginalized communities and drawing attention to their struggles, Dr. Eden sparks important conversations and prompts readers to reevaluate their own roles in the fight against neo-colonialism.

Dr. Getan Eden's profound insights and unwavering commitment to justice have garnered him international recognition and respect. He has become an influential figure in academic circles, policy discussions, and social movements focused on Africa's liberation. Through his extensive research, writings, and speaking engagements, Dr. Eden strives to empower African communities and inspire individuals to actively engage in dismantling the structures of exploitation and oppression that continue to hinder Africa's progress.

With his passion, expertise, and unwavering dedication, Dr. Getan Eden continues to make invaluable contributions to the discourse surrounding neo-colonialism and the exploitation of Africa's mineral wealth. His works serve as a call to action, inspiring readers to join the movement for a more just and equitable world, where Africa's resources are harnessed for the benefit of its people and where the voices of African communities are uplifted and respected.

Exploiting Africa:

The Ugly Truth About Neocolonialism

Contents:

Introduction:

Welcome to a heartfelt exploration of the intricate dynamics surrounding neocolonialism in Africa. In these pages, we embark on a journey to uncover the harsh realities faced by the African continent—a place of immense beauty and untapped potential that has long suffered from exploitation and oppression.

Africa, with its abundant natural resources, has been a target of exploitation for centuries. Although colonialism officially ended, neocolonialism has silently taken its place. Powerful nations wield their economic and political influence to exploit Africa and its people. The remnants of colonialism are still visible today, manifested in the form of poverty, underdevelopment, and political instability.

This book serves as a powerful tool to expose the ugly truth about neocolonialism in Africa. Through a combination of emotional storytelling and factual analysis, we will navigate the historical roots of colonization in Africa and how they laid the foundation for the ongoing exploitation we witness today. We will unravel the rise of neocolonialism and unravel how world superpowers have meticulously exercised their control over African economies and the extraction of valuable minerals from the continent.

With empathy and unwavering determination, we will explore the far-reaching negative impacts of neocolonialism on African economies. We will uncover the deceptive language surrounding aid and investment, exposing the hidden agendas that hinder true progress. We will confront the environmental consequences of mineral extraction and advocate for sustainable practices that preserve Africa's natural heritage.

No discussion of neocolonialism would be complete without addressing the exploitation of African labor and the communities affected. Through personal narratives and profound insights, we will shed light on the injustices faced by African workers and emphasize the urgent need for fair labor practices and community empowerment.

Throughout these pages, we will not only uncover the grim realities but also focus on solutions. This book is a testament to the resilience and agency of the African people. We will emphasize the importance of African voices and agency in achieving economic independence. Genuine partnerships and fair trade will be highlighted as crucial pathways toward dismantling neocolonialism.

As we approach the conclusion of this book, we
invite you to join us in answering the call to action.
This is not just a call to Africans; it is a call to the
global community. We all bear a responsibility to acknowledge
and confront the reality of
neocolonialism in Africa. By working together, we
can strive for a more just and equitable world,
where the exploitation and oppression of the
African continent and its people become a thing of
the past.

Join us as we embark on this transformative
journey, guided by compassion, understanding, and a shared
vision for a better future. Together, we can make a difference and
pave the way for a more equitable world where Africa's true
potential can flourish.

Chapter 1: Unearthing the Enduring Scars of Colonialism

Welcome to Chapter 1, where we embark on a
profound and enlightening exploration of the
profound scars left by colonialism on the vibrant
tapestry of the African continent. Africa, a land with a rich history
and diverse cultures, flourished long before the arrival of
European colonial powers.
However, the arrival of these powers in the late 19th century
marked a somber turning point, subjecting
Africa to a dark era of exploitation, oppression, and
cultural erasure.

The impact of colonization on Africa was deep and
far-reaching, reverberating through generations.
The transatlantic slave trade ripped apart families
and communities, inflicting immeasurable pain and suffering on
millions of Africans. European powers carved up Africa without
regard for the intricate ethnic and linguistic boundaries that had
shaped the continent for centuries. As they plundered Africa's
abundant resources, fueling the industrialization of Europe, Africa
was left impoverished and depleted.

Even today, the scars of colonialism remain visible
across the African landscape. Many nations grapple
with the lingering effects of poverty, political

instability, and social unrest, all stemming from the legacy of their colonial past. Forced labor and displacement shattered the fabric of traditional societies, eroding cultural knowledge and practices that had thrived for generations. The introduction of Christianity and Western education disrupted indigenous belief systems, severing the connection to ancestral heritage.

Yet, in the face of immense adversity, African peoples have exhibited remarkable resilience and unyielding resistance. Visionary leaders such as Samori Ture and Nzinga Mbande, alongside the pan-African movements of the 20th century, have tirelessly fought for the freedom and dignity of their people. However, the enduring scars of colonization and the persistence of neocolonialism serve as poignant reminders that the struggle for true liberation continues.

In the pages of this book, we embark on a captivating journey through the annals of African history, unearthing the profound impact of colonization and its enduring consequences. We shine a light on the ongoing exploitation of the continent by global superpowers, while also illuminating the inspiring stories of African

resistance and resilience. Furthermore, we delve
deep into the emotional toll inflicted by colonization and the
unwavering quest for liberation and dignity that reverberates
throughout Africa.

Together, let us bear witness to the indelible scars of colonialism,
acknowledging the immense challenges that African peoples have
faced and continue to confront. Let us also honor their
unwavering spirit, their tenacity, and their unyielding pursuit of a
brighter future. By embracing a collective understanding of
Africa's past, we pave the way for a future rooted in justice,
equality, and the celebration of Africa's rich heritage.

Beyond the immediate impact on political
structures and economic exploitation, colonialism
engendered a lasting legacy of inequality and
systemic injustice.

One of the most profound effects of colonial rule
was the disruption of African societies and the
fragmentation of cultural identities. European
powers imposed their own systems of governance,
eroding traditional leadership structures and
exacerbating divisions among ethnic groups. This
deliberate strategy aimed to weaken African unity
and maintain control over the colonized territories.

The scars of colonialism also manifested in the form of land dispossession and forced labor. Indigenous populations were forcibly displaced from their ancestral lands, leading to widespread loss of livelihoods and cultural displacement. Additionally, the exploitative labor practices imposed by colonial powers, such as the extraction of resources and the establishment of plantations, further entrenched patterns of economic inequality and exploitation.

Furthermore, colonial education systems were designed to perpetuate the subjugation of African peoples. The curriculum centered on European values, languages, and histories, while marginalizing indigenous knowledge and erasing African contributions to human civilization. This systematic erasure of African cultural heritage and intellectual achievements perpetuated a sense of inferiority among African populations.

In this chapter, we explore the multifaceted impacts of colonialism on African societies, shedding light on the deep-rooted inequalities that persist today. We examine the enduring consequences of land dispossession, forced labor, and educational marginalization. Moreover, we highlight the resilience and agency of African communities in reclaiming their identities, revitalizing cultural practices, and challenging oppressive systems.

It is crucial to recognize that the scars of colonialism are not relics of the past, but living realities that shape the present. Neocolonial structures and power dynamics continue to perpetuate economic exploitation, political instability, and cultural marginalization. To address these ongoing injustices, we must engage in critical reflection, center African perspectives, and work towards dismantling systems that perpetuate inequality.

We can also draw inspiration from the numerous liberation movements and anti-colonial struggles that have shaped Africa's history. From the resistance efforts of figures like Kwame Nkrumah, Jomo Kenyatta, and Amílcar Cabral to the pan-African ideals championed by leaders such as Julius Nyerere and Thomas Sankara, African peoples have consistently fought for self-determination, freedom, and dignity.

As we navigate the complex legacy of colonialism, it is imperative that we confront the scars it has left behind and work toward healing, justice, and reconciliation. By amplifying African voices,

supporting grassroots initiatives, and challenging
systems of oppression, we can contribute to a future where the
wounds of the past are acknowledged, and Africa's diverse
cultures, histories, and contributions are celebrated.

The scars left by colonialism are not confined to the
past; they persist in the present and shape the
socio-economic and political landscape of Africa.
One of the most profound consequences of
colonialism is the legacy of economic exploitation
and dependency. European powers plundered
Africa's natural resources, leaving behind devastated ecosystems
and impoverished
communities. The unequal trade relationships
established during the colonial era continue to
disadvantage African economies, perpetuating a
cycle of poverty and underdevelopment.

Colonialism also entrenched racial hierarchies and
discriminatory ideologies that continue to shape
power dynamics in Africa. The racial divisions
imposed by colonial powers fostered deep-seated
social inequalities and reinforced systems of
oppression. These divisions, along with the artificial borders
drawn by colonial mapmakers, have contributed to conflicts and
tensions among African nations.

Moreover, colonialism left a lasting impact on
governance structures, leading to political instability and
authoritarian regimes.
The imposition of arbitrary borders and the installation of puppet
governments sowed the seeds of division and strife. Many African
nations continue to grapple with the legacy of corrupt leadership,
limited democratic participation, and human rights abuses.

Delve into the complexities of post-colonial Africa, examining the
persistent challenges and the ongoing struggles for self-
determination and equality. We shed light on the efforts of African
leaders and grassroots movements to challenge neocolonial
structures and forge a path toward inclusive governance,
economic empowerment, and social justice.

It is essential to recognize the resilience and agency
of African people in the face of these challenges.
From the anti-apartheid movement in South Africa
to the independence struggles across the continent,
Africans have consistently demonstrated their
determination to overcome the legacy of colonialism and build a
brighter future.

As we navigate the scars of colonialism, we must
also acknowledge the importance of international
solidarity and support. Addressing deep-rooted

injustices requires a collective effort that goes beyond national boundaries. Global recognition of historical injustices and an active commitment to equitable partnerships can contribute to a more just and inclusive world.In this chapter, we invite readers to critically engage with the impact of colonialism, confront the ongoing challenges faced by African nations, and join in the call for justice and empowerment. By amplifying African voices, promoting economic self-sufficiency, and fostering meaningful collaborations, we can work towards a future where Africa reclaims its rightful place as a vibrant, thriving continent.

Join us as we continue to uncover the multifaceted impacts of colonialism and explore the pathways toward liberation, justice, and a more equitable Africa. Through understanding, empathy, and collective action, we can forge a brighter future that respects the inherent dignity and self-determination of all African peoples.

Chapter 2: Unmasking Ongoing Exploitation in Africa

In Chapter 2, we boldly expose the distressing truth that despite the end of colonialism, Africa remains ensnared in the clutches of ongoing exploitation by global superpowers. Multinational corporations, predominantly hailing from developed nations, continue to extract Africa's bountiful natural resources, reaping substantial profits while offering meager benefits to local communities. This insatiable plundering of resources like oil, gold, and diamonds wreaks havoc on the environment, leaving scars that run deep within African communities.

Regrettably, the global economic system perpetuates an unjust trade and financial framework that tilts the scales against African countries. Imposed debt burdens and structural adjustment policies, enforced by international financial institutions, dismantle social welfare programs and facilitate the privatization of state-owned enterprises, further exacerbating poverty and inequality across the continent.

Yet, the neocolonial exploitation of Africa extends
far beyond economic boundaries; it casts a dark
shadow over the political landscape as well. Foreign governments
often meddle in African affairs, bolstering authoritarian regimes
while suppressing democratic movements. The arms trade and
military training provided to African governments fuel conflicts,
breed instability, and force millions of people into displacement.

The persistent exploitation of Africa evokes a
profound moral outrage, demanding swift attention
and concerted action from the global community. It
is high time we recognize and honor the shared
humanity and intrinsic dignity of African peoples.
The voices of African activists and leaders, who
tirelessly champion justice and equality, must
resound with amplified clarity, and their pleas must find attentive
ears.
The world must confront the harm inflicted upon Africa and
actively collaborate to establish a more equitable global system
that respects the rights and aspirations of all nations.

Together, let us stand in unwavering solidarity with
Africa, championing a world where empowerment
eclipses exploitation and fairness triumph over
greed. By acknowledging the profound injustices
and amplifying the voices of change, we can pave a

path toward a future where Africa's abundant resources serve its people, and where a truly just and equitable world blossoms.

With resolute determination, we journey forward, fully committed to shedding light on the path of change and transformation. In this chapter, we delve deeper into the multifaceted dimensions of Africa's ongoing exploitation, exploring its nuanced complexities and far-reaching consequences.
As we peel back the layers, we encounter stories of resilience, resistance, and remarkable courage. African communities, in the face of persistent exploitation, have stood tall, forging bonds of solidarity and unity. Grassroots movements have emerged, fueled by the indomitable spirit of individuals who refuse to accept a future shackled by exploitation.

Women, in particular, have played a pivotal role in challenging the status quo. Their voices reverberate with unwavering determination, advocating for gender equality, inclusive governance, and sustainable development. Their tireless efforts empower communities, paving the way for a more equitable and just society.

Amidst the challenges, Africa's youth have risen as
catalysts of change. Armed with innovative ideas,
they embrace technology and grassroots mobilization to amplify
their voices and reshape the narrative of their continent. Their
energy and
passion infuse hope into the fight against exploitation, igniting a
collective spirit of transformation.

But the struggle for justice and dignity in Africa
cannot be fought alone. It requires global solidarity and
cooperation. It necessitates a paradigm shift in the hearts and
minds of individuals worldwide, fostering empathy and a genuine
commitment to dismantling systems of exploitation.

Explore the interconnectedness of Africa's struggle with broader
global movements for justice and equality. From environmental
activism to indigenous rights movements, we witness the
convergence of struggles, united by a shared vision of a better
world. The fight against exploitation in Africa is not isolated—it is
a battle that transcends borders, demanding collective action.

Together, we must heed the call to action. Let us
amplify the voices of African activists, listening
intently to their wisdom and experiences. Let us
forge alliances, bridge divides, and stand shoulder-
to-shoulder in solidarity with the people of Africa.

By doing so, we can pave the way for a future where exploitation is replaced with empowerment, where justice and equality reign supreme.

In the chapters that follow, we will continue our exploration, uncovering the untold stories, celebrating the triumphs, and reaffirming our unwavering commitment to a just and equitable Africa—a continent where the scars of exploitation are healed, and where the resilience and vibrancy of its people shine brightly for generations to come.

Chapter 3: The Resistance of African Peoples - Illuminating the Spirit of Liberation

In Chapter 3, we embark on a captivating journey, casting a radiant light upon the indomitable spirit and unwavering resilience of African peoples amidst ongoing exploitation. Throughout history, individuals and communities across Africa have risen against oppression, fearlessly advocating for their freedom and asserting their dignity. From the mighty pan-African movements of the 20th century to the impassioned protests and transformative social movements of today, Africans have consistently showcased their unwavering determination to create a world of profound change.

The resistance efforts of African peoples have assumed a multitude of forms, ranging from armed struggles for liberation to the powerful forces of nonviolent resistance. The courageous footsteps of revered leaders like Nelson Mandela, Patrice Lumumba, and Thomas Sankara have left an indelible mark, inspiring generations with their resolute commitment to freedom and the pursuit of dignity. Moreover, the resounding voices of women and young people have played an instrumental role in challenging entrenched patriarchal norms, championing gender equality, and igniting a transformative vision for a more inclusive and just society.

Significantly, the impact of African resistance transcends national boundaries, resonating powerfully on a global scale. African activists and leaders have been catalysts in the worldwide struggle for justice and equality, leaving an enduring legacy that echoes far beyond the continent's borders. From the anti-apartheid movement that galvanized hearts worldwide to the fierce fight against climate change, African voices have fueled and guided transformative social movements across continents.

Within this chapter, we embark on a remarkable voyage through the rich tapestry of Africanresistance, unraveling its profound historical roots and its unwavering reverberations in the present. We delve deep into the remarkable contributions of women and young people in the liberation struggle, honoring their pivotal role in shaping a future illuminated by hope. We also explore the interconnectedness between African struggles and global social movements, weaving together the common threads that bind diverse movements in a collective quest for justice and equality.

While African activists and leaders face ongoing challenges and obstacles, their indomitable spirit remains unyielding. They deserve our unwavering support, solidarity, and recognition. By standing shoulder to shoulder with them and amplifying their resounding voices, we foster a global community that embraces the timeless principles of justice, equality, and the inherent dignity of every human being.

Together, let us celebrate the resounding triumphs of African resistance, drawing inspiration from the 30tapestry of the past and present. By honoring the remarkable struggles of African peoples and nurturing genuine solidarity, we pave the way for a future where the vibrant essence of Africa flourishes, where every voice resounds and every life is cherished.

We immerse ourselves in the captivating stories and remarkable victories of African resistance, where the spirit of liberation burns brightly. We pay homage to the unwavering resolve and unwavering commitment of African peoples who have valiantly confronted oppression and fought for a better future.

The tapestry of African resistance is woven with threads of courage, determination, and sacrifice. It spans diverse landscapes and encompasses a myriad of struggles. From the battle against colonial rule to the ongoing fight against systemic injustices, Africans have risen as agents of change, challenging the status quo and demanding a world that honors their rights and aspirations.

Throughout history, women have been at the forefront of the African liberation struggle. Their voices, like the resounding echoes of hope, have reverberated across the continent, shaping the course of nations and challenging deeply ingrained gender inequalities. From Winnie Madikizela-Mandela, whose unwavering spirit fueled the anti-apartheid movement in South Africa, to Wangari Maathai, whose environmental activism inspired a generation, African women have carved a path of empowerment and resilience.

Young people, too, have ignited the flames of transformation. With their fervor and unwavering belief in a brighter future, they have mobilized movements for social justice, demanding accountability from those in power and envisioning a world where their voices are not just heard but amplified. From the student uprisings in Soweto to the youth-led movements advocating for climate action, African youth have breathed life into the struggle for a more equitable and sustainable future.

The impact of African resistance extends far beyond the continent's borders. African diaspora communities around the world have contributed to the global fight against injustice, infusing movements with their unique experiences and perspectives. From the civil rights movements in the United States to the anti-colonial struggles in the Caribbean, African diaspora voices have shaped the course of history, challenging systems of oppression and paving the way for progress.

Let us delve into the stories of triumph and resilience, weaving a narrative that honors the profound contributions of African resistance. We explore the interconnectedness of African struggles with global social movements, revealing the common ground that unites disparate struggles in a shared quest for justice and human dignity.

As we navigate these narratives, let us celebrate the triumphs and acknowledge the challenges that persist. Let us amplify the voices of African activists, leaders, and everyday heroes who embody the spirit of resistance. By doing so, we honor their resilience, elevate their causes, and work collectively towards a world where exploitation gives way to empowerment, where fairness triumphs over greed.

Together, let us draw inspiration from the rich tapestry of African resistance, charting a course toward a future that embraces the ideals of justice, equality, and the inherent worth of every individual. Through solidarity, understanding, and action, we can create a world where the scars of colonialism are healed, and the flame of liberation burns ever brighter.

Chapter 4: The Environmental Impact of Resource Extraction

In Chapter 4, we delve into the far-reaching environmental consequences of resource extraction in Africa. The unrelenting quest for Africa's precious natural resources, from minerals to oil, has left an indelible mark on the continent's ecosystems. The extraction processes have unleashed pollution, deforestation, and the destruction of vital wildlife habitats, imperiling biodiversity and pushing numerous plant and animal species to the brink of extinction.

The environmental fallout from resource extraction extends beyond the immediate extraction sites, casting a dark shadow over neighboring communities. The contamination of water sources and the deterioration of air quality have inflicted severe health challenges, compounding the already burdensome struggles faced by these communities. Additionally, the loss of traditional livelihoods, such as farming and fishing, has deepened poverty and exacerbated food insecurity, perpetuating a cycle of environmental and socio-economic hardship.

Recognizing the urgency of the situation, it is
imperative for the global community to confront the
environmental ramifications of resource extraction
in Africa. This necessitates the implementation of robust
regulations to hold multinational corporations accountable for their
actions.
Moreover, supporting sustainable development
initiatives that prioritize environmental protection
and the well-being of local communities is of
paramount importance.

Here, we emphasize the vital need to
amplify the voices of African communities most
impacted by environmental degradation. By
centering their perspectives, we can foster a more
inclusive and informed dialogue on ecological
policies and practices. It is essential to recognize the
inseparable link between environmental and social
justice, championing a comprehensive and
equitable approach to development.
Together, we must embrace our role as stewards of
the Earth, prioritizing the preservation of Africa's
natural wonders and the flourishing of its diverse
communities. Through the adoption of sustainable
practices, the cultivation of ecological resilience,
and the empowerment of local voices, we can forge

a path toward a future where Africa's awe-inspiring landscapes thrive harmoniously with the aspirations and needs of its people.

We shift our focus to the critical role of collaboration and international cooperation in addressing the environmental impact of resource extraction in Africa. The challenges faced by African nations require a collective effort from the global community to mitigate and reverse the damage inflicted on the continent's precious ecosystems. International partnerships should prioritize capacity-building initiatives that enable African countries to effectively manage their natural resources while safeguarding the environment. This includes sharing knowledge and expertise in sustainable extraction techniques, environmental monitoring, and the implementation of stringent environmental regulations. By equipping African nations with the necessary tools and resources, we can foster responsible resource management practices that balance economic development with ecological preservation.

Moreover, it is crucial to promote inclusive dialogue and participatory decision-making processes that involve all stakeholders, including local communities, indigenous peoples, and civil society organizations. Their invaluable traditional knowledge and lived experiences can inform strategies for sustainable resource extraction and environmental protection. By centering the voices of those directly affected, we ensure that environmental policies and practices are rooted in the realities and needs of the people on the ground.

Furthermore, efforts to address the environmental impact of resource extraction in Africa should be complemented by broader initiatives that promote renewable energy, green technologies, and sustainable development practices. By diversifying energy sources and investing in clean technologies, we can reduce reliance on extractive industries that harm the environment and contribute to climate change. This transition towards a more sustainable and resilient future will not only benefit Africa but also contribute to global efforts to combat climate change and protect the planet.

In conclusion, Chapter 4 sheds light on the environmental consequences of resource extraction in Africa and emphasizes the need for collaborative action. By engaging in partnerships, empowering local communities, and promoting sustainable practices, we can mitigate the damage caused by resource extraction and pave the way for a more ecologically balanced and equitable future. Let us work together to safeguard Africa's natural heritage and ensure a thriving planet for generations to come.

Chapter 5: Cultural Exploitation and Erasure

In Chapter 5, we delve into the often-overlooked issue of cultural exploitation and erasure faced by Africa. The vibrant and diverse cultures of Africa have been subjected to commodification and appropriation in the global market, perpetuating harmful stereotypes and diminishing the voices of African people.

Cultural exploitation can be observed in industries such as fashion and entertainment, where African styles, music, and art are often appropriated without proper recognition or compensation. This not only erodes the authenticity of African cultures but also reinforces power imbalances and marginalizes African voices.

It is crucial for the global community to acknowledge the importance of preserving and promoting African cultures.
This requires recognizing the value of African cultural products and ensuring fair recognition and compensation for their creators. Supporting initiatives that prioritize the preservation and celebration of African cultures is also vital.

Confronting the historical context of colonialism and neocolonialism is essential in understanding the erasure of African cultures. By centering African voices in discussions about cultural representation and appropriation, we can challenge stereotypes and foster a more nuanced understanding of Africa's rich cultural tapestry.

Through the championing of cultural preservation, equitable representation, and the empowerment of African communities, we can work towards a future that values and respects the diverse contributions of African cultures. Let us celebrate the vibrancy and resilience of African heritage and create a world where cultural diversity is embraced, respected, and cherished. Together, we can ensure that African cultures thrive and continue to enrich the global cultural landscape.

Cultural exploitation and erasure perpetuate harmful narratives about Africa and its people. The appropriation of African cultures not only diminishes their value but also reinforces a distorted and one-dimensional representation of the continent. It is imperative that we challenge these harmful practices and work towards a more equitable and respectful approach to cultural exchange.

Education and awareness play a crucial role in addressing cultural exploitation and erasure. By promoting accurate and nuanced portrayals of African cultures, we can dismantle stereotypes and foster a greater understanding and appreciation for the richness and diversity of Africa's heritage. This includes incorporating African perspectives into educational curricula, supporting cultural exchange programs, and encouraging dialogue that promotes mutual respect and understanding.

Furthermore, collaboration and partnership with African artists, scholars, and cultural institutions are vital in promoting authentic representations of African cultures. By providing platforms for African voices to be heard and amplified, we can empower African communities to reclaim their narratives and challenge the dominant narratives imposed upon them.

It is also essential to address the economic disparities that contribute to cultural exploitation. Supporting fair trade practices, ensuring equitable compensation for African artists and creators, and fostering sustainable partnerships are crucial steps in promoting a more just and inclusive cultural landscape.

In conclusion, the recognition and celebration of African cultures are not only a matter of cultural preservation but also a pursuit of justice and equality. By actively confronting cultural exploitation and erasure, we can promote a world where African voices are respected, valued, and given the opportunity to thrive. Together, let us embrace the richness and diversity of African cultures, fostering a global community that cherishes and uplifts the contributions of all its members.

Furthermore, it is crucial to recognize the agency and ownership of African communities in the representation and dissemination of their own cultures. This means providing platforms and resources that allow Africans to tell their own stories and shape their own narratives. By supporting African-owned media outlets, publishing houses, and cultural institutions, we can ensure that African voices have a prominent place in shaping the global discourse on African cultures.

In addition, promoting cultural exchange programs
that facilitate meaningful interactions between
people from diverse backgrounds can foster mutual
respect and appreciation. These programs can
encourage individuals to engage directly with
African communities, learn from their traditions,
and challenge preconceived notions. By fostering
genuine cultural exchange, we can move away from
exploitation and towards a more equitable and
respectful appreciation of African cultures.

It is also essential to address the economic
dimensions of cultural exploitation. African artists, artisans, and
creators should receive fair
compensation and recognition for their cultural contributions.
Fairtrade practices, ethical
collaborations, and responsible tourism can help
ensure that African artists and cultural practitioners
benefit equitably from their creative endeavors. By
promoting economic empowerment and supporting
sustainable livelihoods within cultural industries, we can combat
the economic disparities perpetuated by cultural exploitation.

Ultimately, addressing cultural exploitation and
erasure in Africa requires a comprehensive and
collaborative effort. It demands a shift in global

attitudes, policies, and practices that perpetuate
stereotypes and marginalize African cultures. By promoting cultural
appreciation, respecting the
agency of African communities, and advocating for
fair representation and economic empowerment, we
can foster a world that values and celebrates the
rich tapestry of African cultures.

Together, let us work towards a future where
African cultures are not only protected but
celebrated, where the contributions of African
communities to the global cultural landscape are
recognized and respected. By embracing diversity
and embracing the power of cultural exchange, we
can create a world that is enriched by the vibrant
and diverse heritage of Africa.

Chapter 6: The Empowering Force of Education in African Liberation

In this chapter, we embark on a comprehensive exploration of the transformative power of education in the context of African liberation. Throughout history, education has played a pivotal role in dismantling oppressive systems, nurturing critical consciousness, and empowering African communities to reclaim their identities and shape their destinies.

Education has been a vehicle for resistance against colonialism, neo-colonialism, and other forms of subjugation. Independent schools and universities established by African activists and leaders have become bastions of intellectual and cultural liberation, incubating a generation of scholars, thinkers, and visionaries committed to social justice and self-determination. The educated elite that emerged from these institutions became catalysts for change, leading movements and driving progress across the continent.

Beyond formal schooling, education encompasses a holistic approach that values and incorporates indigenous knowledge, traditional wisdom, and community-based learning. By embracing diverse ways of knowing and empowering African communities to define their own educational practices, we honor the richness and depth of African cultures while fostering a sense of pride, resilience, and self-awareness.

However, the journey towards educational liberation in Africa is not without challenges. Disparities in access, inadequate infrastructure, and limited resources persist, impeding the realization of education's full potential as a force for liberation. It is imperative for governments, international organizations, and local communities to prioritize investment in education, ensuring equitable access and quality education for all.

Education empowers individuals with knowledge, critical thinking skills, and the ability to challenge oppressive systems. It cultivates agency, self-esteem, and a sense of collective responsibility, nurturing active citizens committed to social transformation and sustainable development. By prioritizing education, Africa nurtures a generation of leaders, innovators, and change-makers who will shape the continent's future with vision, empathy, and resilience.

In conclusion, education stands as a beacon of hope and a catalyst for African liberation. It empowers individuals and communities, fosters cultural preservation, and ignites the spirit of resilience and resistance. By investing in education, we invest in the future of Africa, creating a society where every individual has the opportunity to thrive and contribute to a just, equitable, and prosperous continent.

Let us embrace education as a powerful tool of liberation, creating an inclusive and transformative learning environment where African knowledge systems are respected, valued, and integrated.

Together, we can build a future where education serves as the cornerstone of African liberation, enabling the continent to realize its full potential and forge its own path toward a brighter and more equitable tomorrow.

Chapter 7: The Resilience and Triumph of African Resistance

In this chapter, we embark on a profound exploration of the immeasurable power of African resistance, a force that has shaped history and defied the shackles of exploitation and oppression. African peoples have exemplified extraordinary strength, courage, and unwavering determination in their tireless pursuit of justice, liberation, and dignity, both during the era of colonialism and in the ongoing struggle against neo-colonialism.

The annals of African resistance are a testament to the indomitable spirit of individuals and communities who fearlessly confronted injustice, often at great personal risk. From the fiery anti-colonial movements that surged across the continent in the mid-twentieth century to the present-day battles for human rights and social justice, Africans have illuminated the world with their unwavering commitment to freedom and equality.

It is imperative that we elevate the narratives and experiences of African resistance in our discourse on African history and politics. Too often, the prevailing narrative reduces Africa to a passive victim, overlooking the profound legacy of resistance and resilience that has defined African history.

Within the pages of this chapter, we celebrate and honor the countless heroes and heroines who have valiantly fought for justice and liberation. We delve into their remarkable stories, acknowledging their significant contributions and the sacrifices they have made. Furthermore, we examine the ongoing struggles for social justice and human rights in Africa, recognizing the persistent challenges that arise in the face of neocolonialism and global inequalities.

By shining a spotlight on the power of African resistance, we illuminate the extraordinary capacity of African peoples to challenge the status quo, advocate for their rights, and forge a path toward a future characterized by justice, equality, and human dignity. Through a deeper understanding and amplification of the narratives of African resistance, we foster solidarity, inspire transformative change, and build a more inclusive and equitable world for all. Together, let us honor and learn from the

profound legacy of African resistance as we strive
for a future where the voices of the marginalized are
heard, and the triumph of justice prevails.

Chapter 8: Solidarity Across Borders: Building a Global Movement

In Chapter 8, we delve into the profound significance of solidarity across borders in the ongoing struggle for African liberation. The legacy of colonialism and neocolonialism has given rise to a global system of inequality and exploitation, demanding a unified response from individuals and communities worldwide.

Solidarity across borders serves as a powerful pillar in the fight for African liberation. The challenges faced by African peoples are not isolated; they are deeply intertwined with a broader global framework of injustice and inequality. Through collective action and collaboration, we can effectively challenge and dismantle this system of oppression.

Let us explore the immense value of global solidarity in combating colonialism and neocolonialism. We shed light on how collective support and shared struggles have served as crucial strategies in the battle for African liberation. Moreover, we highlight ongoing initiatives aimed at fostering transnational networks of resistance and solidarity.

While acknowledging that cross-border solidarity work can present challenges and tensions, we address important considerations. We delve into issues of cultural differences, power dynamics, and conflicting priorities that may arise in these efforts. By doing so, we strive to cultivate strategies that promote equitable and effective solidarity networks, emphasizing the necessity of centering the voices and experiences of African peoples in these endeavors.

Additionally, we explore the role of technology and social media in fostering global solidarity movements. The digital age has provided new avenues for connecting and mobilizing activists across borders, amplifying their voices, and facilitating the exchange of knowledge and resources.

By amplifying the significance of solidarity across borders, we underscore the imperative of unity and collaboration in dismantling systems of oppression. Together, we can build a future that champions justice, equality, and the liberation of African peoples, while fostering a global community founded on empathy, understanding, and shared humanity. It is through our collective efforts that we pave the way for a world where dignity, freedom, and self-determination flourish for all.

Chapter 9: Charting the Path Forward: The Future of African Liberation

As we conclude this transformative journey, Chapter 9 embarks on an exploration of the possibilities and challenges that lie ahead in the future of African liberation. The struggle for African liberation continues to unfold, and the trajectory of Africa's future is being shaped by the collective efforts of its people.

Within this chapter, we delve into the ongoing struggles for social justice and human rights in Africa, recognizing the enduring impact of neocolonialism and global inequality on African societies. Moreover, we celebrate the powerful legacy of resistance and resilience that defines African history, acknowledging the remarkable efforts made to build more equitable and just societies.

In addition, we examine the pivotal role of the global community in supporting the struggle for African liberation. By recognizing and addressing the ways in which neocolonialism and global inequality perpetuate injustice and exploitation in Africa, we can foster meaningful change. We emphasize the importance of amplifying the voices and leadership of African activists and communities while advocating for a more inclusive and equitable global system that upholds the dignity and humanity of all individuals.

The future of African liberation lies in the hands of African peoples themselves. It is their vision, determination, and agency that will chart the course ahead. As members of the global community, we have a responsibility to listen, learn, and support the aspirations and goals of African activists and communities. By collaborating and working towards sustainable and equitable development initiatives, we can collectively contribute to a future that embraces justice, equality, and the flourishing of African societies.

In this final chapter, we reflect on the resilience and tenacity that have characterized the African liberation struggle. We acknowledge the challenges that lie ahead, including the need for economic empowerment, environmental sustainability, and the preservation of cultural heritage. However, we also embrace the hope and potential for positive change. The future of African liberation is rooted in solidarity, collaboration, and the unwavering commitment to justice.

Together, let us continue to champion the cause of African liberation and stand in solidarity with the people of Africa as they shape their own future. Through our collective efforts, we can forge a path that upholds the values of justice, dignity, and shared prosperity, ensuring that Africa's vibrant tapestry of cultures, environments, and aspirations thrives for generations to come. The journey continues, and the future of African liberation awaits its next chapter.

Epilogue: Answering the Call: Taking Action for African Liberation

As we conclude this transformative journey, the epilogue serves as a poignant reminder that the struggle for African liberation is not a story to be passively observed but a call to action that demands our engagement. It beckons us to step forward with empathy, awareness, and a commitment to effect meaningful change.

We cannot turn a blind eye to the injustices and inequalities faced by African peoples within global systems of power. It is incumbent upon us to recognize our own role in perpetuating these systems and to actively work toward dismantling them. Our actions, both big and small, have the power to shape a more equitable and just world.

At the heart of our efforts lies the imperative to amplify the voices and experiences of African activists and communities. By lending them our ears, learning from their struggles, and becoming true allies, we can collectively forge a path toward liberation and justice.

In embracing this responsibility, we pay tribute to the unwavering spirit of resistance and resilience that defines African history. Together, we can envision a future where every individual, regardless of their background, can thrive in a world characterized by dignity, justice, and freedom. The journey for African liberation continues, and our dedication to collective action and collaboration will be the compass guiding our path.

Let us heed the call to action and commit ourselves to the struggle for African liberation. Through our determination and solidarity, we can create a future that reflects the values of dignity, justice, and freedom. The time for action is now, as we join hands and embark on a journey toward a better world for all.

As we bid farewell to this exploration of African liberation, let us carry with us the stories, the resilience, and the aspirations of the African people. May their struggles inspire us to challenge the status quo, confront systems of oppression, and advocate for a world where justice, equality, and human dignity prevail.

In closing, remember that the power for change
resides within each of us. Together, let us be
catalysts for a future where African liberation is no
longer an aspiration but a reality. With compassion, determination,
and a shared commitment to justice,
we can shape a world that honors the struggles of
the past, respects the present, and builds a brighter,
more equitable future for generations to come.